A GUIDE TO YOUR
Spice
Rack

What to Pinch
When to Dash
Where to Sprinkle

Printed in the United States of America
by G&R Publishing Co.

Published By:

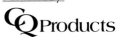

507 Industrial Street
Waverly, IA 50677

ISBN-13: 978-1-56383-315-1
ISBN-10: 1-56383-315-8
Item #7094

Spice it Up!

You know those spice jars taking over your cupboards and drawers? The ones that never stay in alphabetical order and multiply at an alarming rate? The ones that you can't cook without, and the ones that you bought for a new recipe – never to be used again? The ones that bring that familiar flavor to a favorite dish, and the ones that contain something so unusual that you prefer to ignore its existence? Yep, we're talking about spices!

Those little jars, with their hot powders, fragrant herbs and tasty seeds, also contain some fascinating secrets. Those very spices have caused wars to be waged, monopolies to be broken, cultures to be explored, and countries to be discovered!

With this book as your guide, it's time to spice up your life with the fascinating, fragrant, flavor-filled world of zing, zest, punch and pizzazz that is waiting right there in your cupboard. Let's get spicy!

Shelf Life & Storage 4
Spices A-Z .... 5 – 49
Spice Blends .... 50 – 59
Make Your Own! 60

Shelf Life & Storage

Just like that goldenrod shag carpet or pastel-striped couch in your living room, your spice rack needs to be updated every once in awhile. And even though they never technically "go bad", spices and herbs do lose their potency, strength, color and flavor over time. Follow these basic rules about the shelf life of your spices and herbs:

- · Dried, Whole – 2 years
- · Dried, Crushed or Cut – 1 year
- · Ground – 6 months

You will always find fresher, stronger spices at stores where you can package your own portions from larger bins. But it is important to protect your spices, no matter how fresh or new they are. The three culprits that could affect the quality of your spices are heat, light and moisture. Always keep your spices away from sources of heat in your kitchen, such as a stove or dishwasher. Try to keep your spices inside dark, air-tight containers or jars – away from windows and other bright areas. And finally, always close and replace your spice jars and containers after use. However, spices from the red pepper family (paprika, cayenne and chili powder) will remain fresher and retain their color when stored in the refrigerator.

Toasting Tip

Some spices (namely cumin seeds, coriander seeds, mustard seeds, fennel seeds, poppy seeds and sesame seeds) benefit from being toasted or dry-roasted to accentuate their taste and aroma. Heat a heavy, dry skillet over medium heat until hot. Add the spice and toast, stirring constantly, for 2 to 5 minutes, or until the spice is fragrant and/or lightly browned; remove from heat.

Allspice

What you'll find on the spice rack:

- **Whole:** dark, reddish brown pea-size spheres with a rough surface
- **Ground:** rich, dark brown powdered spice with a warm aroma

Common uses:

- The majority of the world's allspice harvest is used in commercial ketchups and sauces.
- Allspice is popular in seasoning blends, especially jerk seasoning, as well as apple pie spice and pumpkin spice.

What is it?

Allspice is a dried unripe berry from the Pimenta dioica tree, a small West Indian tree that grows about 30 feet tall. It has fragrant green leaves and white flowers that blossom into the allspice fruit. When dried, allspice berries can be used whole or ground into a powder. It takes 5 whole berries to equal 1 teaspoon of ground allspice. Allspice is mistakenly thought to be a spice blend because it contains the aroma of several spices (cloves, pepper, cinnamon and nutmeg), which also explains the origin of its name.

Try it this way:

- Sprinkle over cottage cheese, deviled eggs, or custards.
- Simmer whole allspice berries in mulled cider; remove before serving.
- Mix ⅛ teaspoon ground allspice per 1 pound of ground beef to make meatloaf or hamburgers.

Aniseed

What you'll find on the spice rack:

+ **Whole:** tiny leaf- or crescent-shaped seeds in a dull greenish-brown color with a sweet taste and a licorice-almond scent
+ **Ground:** a coarse yellow powder with a sweet licorice flavor

Common uses:

+ The whole seeds are chewed after meals in India to sweeten the breath.
+ Ground seeds are used in breads, cakes and confections in Europe and the Middle East to add sweetness.
+ Whole seeds are stirred into pizza sauces to enhance flavor.

What is it?

Anise is a flowering plant from southwest Asia and the eastern Mediterranean region. It is a member of the parsley family. The plant grows to about 3 feet and sprouts two types of leaves. The upper feathery leaves contain the dry fruit, which splits open when mature to reveal the aniseed. Both the leaves and seeds of anise contain the anethole oil that gives them a sweet licorice taste.

Try it this way:

+ Use whole aniseed to make Chicken Mole, a Mexican favorite.
+ Crushed aniseed is necessary for preparing a proper French-style Pain d'épice, commonly called Spice Bread or Honey Bread.
+ Stir 1 teaspoon of crushed aniseed into a cup of boiling water; steep for 10 minutes. Drink this tea after a meal as a digestive aid.

Do not confuse aniseed with star anise (described on page 44). Though they are similar in taste and name, they are completely separate spices.

Basil

What you'll find on the spice rack:

+ **Crushed:** bright greenish-brown dried flakes with a fragrant, hay-like and somewhat bitter flavor and scent

Common uses:

+ Basil is a prominent ingredient in Italian cuisine and pairs well with most tomato dishes, including soups, pizza, pasta and casseroles.
+ Dried basil is often mixed with oils and vinegars to make salad dressings and marinades.
+ Fresh basil is one of the main ingredients in pesto, giving the oil-and-herb sauce its green hue.

What is it?

Basil is an herb from the Lamiaceae family, which also includes mint, oregano, catnip, rosemary and sage. Basil plants can vary in height from 8 inches to 3 feet. There are several types of basil, including Lemon Basil and Holy Basil, though the most popular is the Italian favorite, Sweet Basil. It is believed that basil originated in India, but it is now cultivated worldwide and has become a favorite herb for home gardeners. Crushed basil is made by drying and crumbling fresh, silky basil leaves.

Try it this way:

+ Sprinkle dried basil over tomato slices and fresh mozzarella.
+ Make a basil cream sauce for chicken or seafood by combining a pinch of dried basil with light cream, Parmesan cheese, minced garlic, olive oil, salt and pepper; stir over medium heat until the cheese is melted.
+ Stir dried basil into dough before baking breads, biscuits and rolls.

Bay Leaves

What you'll find on the spice rack:

+ **Whole:** crisp, dried, olive green leaves with a much stronger flavor and fragrance than fresh bay leaf
+ **Crushed:** dull green, dried flakes with a distinct fragrance, can be crushed at home from whole dried leaves or bought in crushed form

Common uses:

+ The famous head wreaths worn by Greek scholars were often made from bay leaves.
+ Fresh or dried whole bay leaf is frequently used in a bouquet garni (a tied bundle of herbs) to flavor soups, stews and sauces, then removed before serving.

What is it?

Bay is a warm-climate, perennial, evergreen shrub with shiny, smooth leaves. It also thrives as a container herb when pruned and properly mulched. Laurus nobilis is the most popular type of bay, though California and Indian Bay Leaf are also common in the U.S. One type of bay leaf, Mountain laurel, is poisonous to certain livestock. This led to the mistaken belief that bay leaf might be poisonous to humans and should be removed before eating. Though none of the commercial brands are poisonous, it is still desirable to remove whole bay leaves from dishes before serving, but only because they could be a choking hazard.

Try it this way:

+ Drop a whole bay leaf into homemade soup or tomato sauce; remove before serving.
+ Sprinkle crushed bay leaf into bean dishes for flavor.
+ Add whole bay leaves to a bowl of water with floating candles to release a wonderful fragrance throughout the home.

Capers

What you'll fiind on the spice rack:

+ **Pickled:** small, olive green, dried buds preserved in a salt and vinegar solution

Common uses:

+ Capers are very popular in southern Italian cuisine for use on pizzas, in salads and pasta sauces.
+ Often, capers are ground into tapenades and savory spreads.
+ Capers are an essential ingredient in Chicken Piccata and Pasta Puttanesca, popular Italian dishes.

What is it?

Capers are the unripened flower buds of a Mediterranean, prickly perennial plant, the Capparis spinosa. The buds are harvested, dried in the sun, then pickled to bring out a tangy, salty, lemony flavor, similar to that of green olives. The buds range in size from tiny peas to small olives. The smaller the caper, the more expensive and prized it becomes. Capers out of the jar can be overwhelmingly salty, so it may be desirable to rinse them quickly in a small strainer under running water before adding them to a dish.

Try it this way:

+ Use capers in place of olives in a dry martini.
+ Serve capers with cream cheese and cold, smoked salmon or lox; assemble on bagels, bread or crackers.
+ Stir capers into potato or pasta salads to add a spicy, salty flavor.

Always store an opened jar of capers (or any jar of pickled seasoning) in the refrigerator instead of the spice rack.

Caraway Seed

What you'll find on the spice rack:

+ **Whole:** tiny, crescent-shaped dried fruits (not seeds) with a greenish-brown hue and pale ridges
+ **Ground:** sweet and spicy, pale reddish-brown powder

Common uses:

+ Caraway seed is the dominant flavor used in many kinds of rye bread.
+ Ground caraway is often used to season sauerkraut and other cabbage-based foods.
+ Whole and ground caraway is a common flavoring in many cheese sauces and specialty cheeses, especially Havarti.

What is it?

Caraway seed is the fruit of the Carum carvi plant but is often mistaken for a seed, hence the name. The fruits have a pungent, anise-like flavor. The majority of the world's caraway is produced in Holland, as well as Egypt and Germany. In addition to culinary uses, the oil from caraway seed is often used as a fragrance component in soaps, lotions and perfumes.

Try it this way:

+ Mix 1 to 2 teaspoons of whole caraway seed into ¼ cup of melted butter; pour over steamed vegetables.
+ Stir ground caraway seed into spice cake batter before baking.
+ Stir 1 teaspoon of whole caraway seed into a 1-quart jar of pickles to mimic a barrel-cured flavor; let sit for 1 day before serving.

Cardamom

What you'll find on the spice rack:

+ **Pod:** generally brown or green, sometimes bleached white, whole dried pods plucked when three-quarters ripe, containing the cardamom seeds inside
+ **Ground:** brown or black powder made from grinding the cardamom seeds

Common uses:

+ In Middle Eastern countries, ground cardamom is used to flavor coffee for visiting guests.
+ In Scandinavian cooking, cardamom is used in sweet pastries and bread, similar to the American use of cinnamon.
+ Cardamom is used in several spice blends, most notably in garam masala.

What is it?

Cardamom, a member of the ginger family, comes in two popular varieties. Elettaria, or green cardamom, is distributed mainly from India and Guatemala, while Amomum, or black cardamom, is distributed mainly from Asia and Australia. Though the pods are not eaten, it is often desirable to purchase cardamom in pod form because the seeds quickly lose their flavor after being exposed or ground. Because the harvesting of cardamom is labor intensive, it follows saffron and vanilla on the list of most expensive spices. It generally takes 10 pods to equal 1½ teaspoons of ground cardamom.

Try it this way:

+ Grind a few cardamom seeds and add to a rice dish, soup or pâté .
+ Sprinkle a few cardamom seeds or a pinch of ground cardamom over fresh fruit, ice cream or custard.

Cayenne Pepper

What you'll find on the spice rack:

+ **Whole:** dried, spicy, red chile peppers, about 2 to 5 inches long; sometimes crushed into red pepper flakes
+ **Ground:** sifted, spicy and potent red pepper powder

Common uses:

+ Ground cayenne pepper, or the seeds from dried whole peppers, is used to intensify the heat in salsas or taco sauces.
+ Cayenne pepper is common in Mexican cuisine to marinate and spice meat.
+ Whole dried cayenne peppers are used in Szechuan cooking to make popular dishes, such as Kung Pao Chicken and Stir-Fried Beef.

What is it?

The spice cayenne pepper, also called red pepper, is the ground form of a dried, cayenne chile pepper or many other red spicy peppers. Whole cayenne chile peppers are harvested, dried and sold whole. However, the majority of cayenne chiles are used to make ground cayenne pepper.

Try it this way:

+ Stir a pinch of cayenne pepper into vegetable dips, salad dressings or tartar sauce to add a little spice.
+ Add a kick to your omelet or scrambled eggs by stirring in a little cayenne pepper or red pepper flakes.
+ Dissolve a very small pinch of ground cayenne pepper in a glass of water, or boil a whole cayenne pepper in water; gargle to help relieve a sore throat.

Do not confuse cayenne pepper with chili powder (described on page 51). Though they are similar in color, chili powder is a spice blend and much hotter than cayenne pepper.

Celery Seed

What you'll find on the spice rack:

+ **Whole:** tiny, greenish-brown seeds with a strong celery-like flavor and aroma

Common uses:

+ For medicinal purposes, celery seed has long been used as a diuretic to help clear toxins from the body, as well as a pain reliever for gout and rheumatoid arthritis.
+ Celery seed is used in many spice blends, including celery salt, pickling spices and curry blends.

What is it?

Celery seed is the dried fruit of the Apium graveolens plant. It is very similar, but not identical, to the celery plant well known for the vegetable celery. The plants grow to about 3 feet with segmented leaves and small white flowers, which contain the celery seed. Most celery seed comes from China, India and France. Indian celery seed has the strongest flavor and is considered the premium choice, while Chinese and French types are milder. Use celery seed sparingly to avoid overpowering a dish.

Try it this way:

+ Stir a little celery seed into coleslaw or cold pasta salad.
+ Whip up a batch of boxed or homemade macaroni and cheese, then stir in a 14.5-ounce can of drained stewed tomatoes and ¼ teaspoon celery seed.
+ Sprinkle a little celery seed over a fish fillet or cut of beef before grilling.

The popular spice blend celery salt is a combination of ground celery seed and salt. It is a famous flavoring for Bloody Mary cocktails and sprinkling over Chicago-style hot dogs.

Chives

What you'll find on the spice rack:

+ ***Freeze-Dried:*** chopped, bright green chive leaves immediately freeze-dried after harvesting, with a delicate, peppery-onion flavor and a hint of garlic

Common uses:

+ Chives are frequently used in potato dishes, such as mashed potatoes or Shepherd's Pie.
+ Chives are often used as a topping or garnish for baked potatoes, as well as bowls of chili and cream-based soups.

What is it?

Chives are the smallest and mildest species of the onion family Alliaceae. A bulb-forming perennial, chive plants grow about 1 to 2 feet tall. The hollow, tubular leaves are soft and straight and produce pale purple, star-shaped flowers. The straight leaves are usually the only part cultivated for culinary uses, however, the flowers can be used as a garnish or in ornamental dried bouquets. Chives should always be added late in the cooking process, since heat lessens their mild flavor.

Try it this way:

+ Jazz up store-bought dips by stirring in a tablespoon of freeze-dried chives.
+ Sauté freeze-dried chives with shrimp or other seafood.
+ Add a sprinkling of freeze-dried chives to almost any salad, soup, egg dish or potato dish.

Cilantro

What you'll find on the spice rack:

+ **Crushed:** light green, dried flakes with a strong earthy scent, but with slightly less bitter taste than fresh cilantro

Common uses:

+ Cilantro is a common ingredient in many salsas and Mexican sauces.
+ In the Middle East, cilantro leaves are used to flavor pickles, curries and chutneys.

What is it?

Cilantro is the American name for the leaves and stem of the coriander herb plant, Coriandrum sativum. The entire plant is edible, including the seeds, which are known as the spice coriander. Cilantro is one of the fastest growing herbs. It is desirable to harvest the ruffled cilantro leaves when they are small, as the leaves get a stronger, sometimes disagreeable flavor as they grow older and larger.

Try it this way:

+ Use dried cilantro to season any Mexican recipe, from salsa and guacamole to tacos and burritos.
+ Sprinkle dried cilantro over pasta dishes with tomato and cream-based sauces.
+ Mix dried cilantro into marinades for chicken, tofu or beef, or into sauces for noodles or leafy salads.
+ Blend a pinch of dried cilantro into melted butter and brush over corn on the cob or chicken on the grill.

Cinnamon

What you'll find on the spice rack:

+ *Stick:* reddish-brown, coiled quills of inner bark with a spicy sweet flavor and festive, warm aroma
+ *Ground:* reddish-brown powder, stronger in scent and flavor than cinnamon sticks

Common uses:

+ Cinnamon is used to flavor a large number of baked goods and is considered a spice of utmost importance to bakers everywhere.
+ Often used to season hot cocoa or coffee, cinnamon is one of the integral ingredients in commercial Chai Tea.
+ Cinnamon is used in a variety of spice blends, including garam masala, jerk seasoning and mulling spices.

What is it?

Cinnamon, one of the oldest and most popular spices, comes from the bark of several varieties of trees in the evergreen family. The most popular type of cinnamon comes from trees of the Cinnamomum cassia type, and is best suited for baking. Cinnamon is graded based on its essential oil content. Those varieties containing higher oil contents, such as the Ceylon or Saigon types, are considered superior. The search for cinnamon was one of the major factors for interest in the exploration of the New World and, therefore, can be partially credited for the discovery of America.

Try it this way:

+ Stir a pinch of cinnamon into homemade or bottled barbecue sauce for a fresh, light flavor accent.
+ Sprinkle a little cinnamon over peaches or pineapple slices cooked on the grill.
+ Mix a little cinnamon into a bowl of meaty chili to balance the heat and complement the beef.

Cloves

What you'll find on the spice rack:

+ **Whole:** small, brown nail-shaped buds with four unopened petals and a small ball in the center
+ **Ground:** brownish-red powder with a warm and sweet aroma and taste

Common uses:

+ Cloves provide the familiar aromatic flavor and taste in gingerbread and pumpkin pie.
+ Whole cloves are often used to stud beef, pork roasts and ham for both flavor and presentation.
+ Cloves pair well with cinnamon and ginger, and are used in many traditional baking recipes.

What is it?

Cloves are picked by hand as unopened pink or red flower buds from the evergreen clove tree in the Myrtaceae family. The clove buds are then dried until they turn brown and hard. Cloves are harvested primarily in Zanzibar, Indonesia and Madagascar, as well as India, Pakistan and Sri Lanka. One of the earliest references to cloves recommended that those who wanted to approach the Chinese emperor should put cloves in their mouths to sweeten the breath.

Try it this way:

+ Pierce an onion with whole cloves; simmer in soup or broth to impart flavor.
+ For an Indian-inspired flavor, add a pinch of ground cloves and curry powder to sautéed onions, garlic and tofu.
+ Stir a bit of ground cloves into a summery fruit salad.

Coriander

What you'll find on the spice rack:

+ **Whole:** yellowish-brown, peppercorn-size spheres with alternating straight and wavy ridges
+ **Ground:** light brown powder with a unique tangy flavor

Common uses:

+ Whole coriander is used in many pickling blends and certain drinks, such as mulled wine.
+ Ground coriander is often used in Scandinavian baking or to flavor soups and curry recipes.
+ Coriander is frequently used in the manufacture of sausages, as well as cigarettes.

What is it?

The spice coriander refers to the dried ripe fruit of the coriander herb plant, Coriandrum sativum. The stem and leaves of the same plant are known in America as the herb cilantro, however, it tastes completely different than coriander. The mildly-fragrant coriander is often described as a combination of lemon, sage and caraway. Most coriander is harvested in Morroco and Romania.

Try it this way:

+ Use coriander seeds in marinades (or ground coriander as a rub) for meat, poultry and seafood.
+ Stir a little ground or whole coriander into sauces, soups and stews for a Mediterranean flavor.
+ Sprinkle some ground coriander over a chopped tomato salad.
+ Add a few coriander seeds to a homemade or store-bought prepared stuffing.

Cream of Tartar

What you'll find on the spice rack:

+ *Ground:* acidic white powder with a thick, silky texture and no aroma

Common uses:

+ Cream of tartar is used to stabilize egg whites in meringues, angel food, soufflés, chiffon cakes and some candies.
+ Occasionally cream of tartar is stirred into frostings and sauces to make them creamier.
+ Cream of tartar is one of the major ingredients in baking powder.

What is it?

Cream of tartar is the natural pure ingredient left behind after grapes have fermented into wine. A crystalline acid forms on the inside of wine barrels. The barrels are scraped, then the sediment is purified and ground to create cream of tartar.

Try it this way:

+ Use cream of tartar as an ant repellent; sprinkle around doorways and cracks, or directly around ant holes.
+ Mix cream of tartar with a little water until a paste forms. Use it to clean rust or dirt from fabrics or silverware.
+ Use the same paste described above to clean a fiberglass or acrylic bathtub. Just spread the paste over soiled areas and scrub with a small brush.
+ When used in recipes for baked goods, cream of tartar acts as a leavening agent to help dough and batter rise.

Cumin

What you'll find on the spice rack:

+ **Whole:** tiny, pale brown, dried seeds with nine ridges and a petite filament growing at one end
+ **Ground:** khaki-colored powder, a little oily in texture with a warm, slightly spicy and sweet flavor, reminiscent of Indian curry

Common uses:

+ Cumin is a popular ingredient for curry powder, as well as other hot blends, including garam masala and African baharat.
+ Cumin is considered a must for making chili con carne and other Tex-Mex dishes.
+ Cumin has long been known for its digestive properties, in addition to many other medicinal purposes.

What is it?

The spice cumin refers to the dried fruit of the cumin plant, an annual herbaceous plant native to the Eastern Mediterranean region. It is from the same plant family as parsley, and related to fennel, coriander and dill. Cumin is an age-old spice that was favored by Ancient Egyptians, Greeks and Romans. It was mentioned several times in both the Old and New Testaments of the Bible. Cumin is now commercially grown in several countries, including Iran, Turkey, Syria, China and Latin America.

Try it this way:

+ Use whole or ground cumin in place of pepper to season any dish.
+ Toast whole cumin in a skillet with a little butter; stir into rice or pour over steamed vegetables.
+ Whisk a little ground cumin into eggs for an omelet.

Dill

What you'll find on the spice rack:

- **Whole Seeds:** light brown seeds with a slightly curved ridged surface and a warming, green flavor
- **Crushed Leaves:** delicate thread-like green leaves that have been dried, crushed and broken, characterized by sweet, grassy, rye-like flavor, more subtle than dill seeds

Common uses:

- Dill is a common flavoring for borscht and other soups, cured salmon and pickles.
- Dill is a popular flavoring for cream-based vegetable dips.
- Dill is often paired with lemon and used in marinades, sauces and rubs for seafood.

What is it?

Dill is an annual herb and sole species of the genus Anethum. Almost every part of the plant can be used, from the seeds (commonly called dill seed) to the leaves (commonly called dill weed). The name dill is believed to have originated from the Norse or Anglo-Saxon word "dilla", meaning to soothe or lull, because the plant was believed to have a calming effect on crying babies. Both dill seed and dill weed have an aroma and flavor similar to caraway.

Try it this way:

- Stir a little dried dill weed into butter; spread over bread, corn, seafood or roasts.
- Sprinkle a generous pinch of dried dill weed over steamed or sautéed vegetables, such as carrots, green beans, onions or asparagus.
- For a stomach-soothing tea, combine 2 teaspoons of crushed dill seed and 1 cup of boiling water; steep for 10 minutes.

Fennel

What you'll find on the spice rack:

+ **Whole Seeds:** light brownish-green, striped, pointed seeds with a flavor and aroma similar to anise
+ **Crushed Leaves:** thin, thread-like leaves with an aromatic hint of black licorice and a flavor similar to dill

Common uses:

+ Fennel is one of the primary ingredients in the liqueur absinthe.
+ Fresh or dried fennel leaves are commonly used in egg and seafood dishes.
+ Fennel is used as a flavoring in some natural toothpastes.

What is it?

Fennel is a perennial herb in the genus Foeniculum and member of the Apiaceae family. It is a hardy plant with a flavorful onion-like white bulb, feathery leaves and dry seeds, all of which can be consumed. Fennel has a strong aroma reminiscent of anise or black licorice, but a flavor that is much sweeter and subdued. Fennel plants grow wild in most parts of temperate Europe, the Mediterranean and India.

Try it this way:

+ Fold 1 teaspoon of fennel seed into ground beef or turkey to make meatballs.
+ Sprinkle dried fennel leaves over a bowl of soup or salad.
+ Combine crushed fennel seed or leaves (or both) with oil and use as a marinade for seafood or pork roasts.
+ For a quick dinner, sauté fennel seed with sliced sausage, onion and peppers; toss with cooked pasta.

Garlic

What you'll find on the spice rack:

+ **Processed:** garlic that has been peeled then sliced, chopped or pressed and preserved in jars with liquid or in paste form
+ **Flaked:** dehydrated garlic bits dried in flake form until hard
+ **Granulated:** dehydrated garlic that has been ground into a cornmeal-like consistency
+ **Ground:** dehydrated garlic that has been ground into a fine yellowish-white powder

Common uses:

+ One of the most potent and popular forms of garlic is the seasoning blend garlic salt, a combination of garlic powder and salt.
+ Garlic in any form is a popular ingredient for salsas, dips, sauces, marinades, casseroles and soups.

What is it?

Garlic is a vegetable from the onion family Alliaceae and closely related to the onion, shallot and leek. Its characteristic scent and flavor have made it one of the world's most popular ingredients, as well as one of the first dehydrated vegetable seasonings. The many different varieties of garlic have different levels of heat and flavor.

Try it this way:

+ Mix minced, granulated or ground garlic with a little butter, lemon juice and minced parsley; spread over bread, biscuits, vegetables or pasta.
+ Sprinkle any form of garlic over chicken, roasts, ribs, pizzas, pasta and shrimp.

Ginger

What you'll find on the spice rack:

+ **Crystallized:** pale orange slices of gingerroot cooked in a sugary syrup until tender, then coated with granulated sugar; also known as candied ginger
+ **Ground:** pale yellowish-orange powder from the ground roots of ginger, with a much milder sweet taste than fresh gingerroot

Common uses:

+ Crystallized ginger is often chopped and added to baked goods or used as a dessert garnish.
+ Ground ginger is a common ingredient in baked goods, such as gingerbread, gingersnaps and ginger cake.

What is it?

Ginger is a tropical perennial plant in the Zingiberaceae family with tangled thick knobby roots and leafy stems that grow about three to four feet high. To harvest gingerroot, the plants are immediately scalded, washed or scraped after the stalks wither, to prevent sprouting. The root is then broken down into smaller pieces for distribution. Ginger is cultivated in China, India, West Africa, Southeast Asia and the Caribbean.

Try it this way:

+ Ginger flavor matches well with fruit, pumpkin, pork, onions, carrots, rice and chicken. Try adding a ¼ teaspoon of ground ginger to basic recipes that include these ingredients.
+ Stir ⅛ teaspoon of ground ginger into a cup of tea to settle nausea or motion sickness.
+ Add finely chopped crystallized ginger to brownie, cookie and biscotti recipes.

Mace

What you'll find on the spice rack:

+ **Whole:** reddish-orange, coarsely chopped mace blades resulting in crisp flakes with citrus, nutmeg and terpeney flavor notes
+ **Ground:** brick-orange coarse powder with a spicy, warming scent

Common uses:

+ Mace is a common ingredient in sausages, ketchup, puddings and donuts.
+ Ground mace is often used in commercially-sold soups, cheeses and cream-based sauces.

What is it?

Mace and nutmeg are both harvested from the Myristica fragrans tree. Mace blades are the thin, bright red, lace-like covering on the shell of the nutmeg. Though its flavor is comparable to nutmeg, mace is much more subdued and delicate. Until the 18th century, Indonesia was the world's only known source for mace, and the majority of the world's supply is still cultivated there. However, other areas are now producing and exporting both mace and nutmeg.

Try it this way:

+ Use ground mace in place of nutmeg in any recipe.
+ Simmer dried mace blades in chicken noodle soup; remove before serving.
+ Liven up mashed potatoes, macaroni and cheese or creamed spinach by stirring in a little ground mace.

Marjoram

What you'll find on the spice rack:

+ **Crushed:** greenish-brown crushed leaves with a warm and aromatic, slightly sharp and bitter flavor
+ **Ground:** grayish-green powder, comparable but slightly sweeter and more delicate flavor than oregano

Common uses:

+ Marjoram is a frequently-used ingredient in Italian, Mediterranean and Middle Eastern foods.
+ Because of its delicate floral aroma, marjoram is often used in soaps, air fresheners and herbal wreaths.

What is it?

Marjoram is made from the dried leaves and floral parts of the herb Origanium hortensis. For a long time, marjoram was considered a wild version of the herb oregano. However, the two plants do not look similar, and marjoram has more of a mild, sweet flavor than oregano with a hint of balsam. Egypt is the principal source for marjoram, but other producers include East Europe, France and the U.S.

Try it this way:

+ Marjoram is often considered *the* herb for flavoring meat. Use it in marinades, rubs and seasonings for your favorite sausages, lamb, beef, pork, poultry and seafood.
+ Stir crushed or ground marjoram into beef stew.
+ Use marjoram to season raw, sautéed or steamed vegetables.
+ Blend crushed marjoram with other spices, namely parsley, dill, basil and thyme; use to season sauces and soups.

Mint

What you'll find on the spice rack:

+ **Crushed:** light to dark green, dried, crushed leaves with a strong aroma and cool, sweet aftertaste

Common uses:

+ Mint is a common flavoring used in teas, beverages, jellies, syrups and ice creams.
+ A classic pairing with chocolate, mint is also used in popular cocktail recipes, such as the Mint Julep, Mojito and Grasshopper.
+ Mint was originally used as a medicinal herb to treat stomach aches and chest pains.

What is it?

There are about 25 known species of mint, a mostly-perennial fast-growing flowering plant in the Lamiaceae family. Peppermint, spearmint and apple mint are the most popular types of mint cultivated for culinary purposes. Peppermint is more often used for candies and teas, while spearmint complements savory dishes like lamb, peas and other vegetables, as well as fruits and chocolate. Other popular types of mint include Swiss mint, Vietnamese mint, English mint, Corsican mint and banana mint. Today, mint is commercially cultivated in the U.S. and Egypt.

Try it this way:

+ Sprinkle dried mint over fruit salads or rice pilaf.
+ Use dried mint in marinades for chicken.
+ A favorite in England, sprinkle dried mint over steamed peas or new potatoes.

Mustard Seed

What you'll find on the spice rack:

+ **Whole:** white, yellow or brown tiny round seeds with
  a fresh, sharp aroma and pungent, slightly biting flavor
+ **Ground:** pale yellow powder, also called dry mustard, with a
  sharp aroma and slightly-less biting flavor than mustard seed

Common uses:

+ Mustard seed is used in pickling spices for vegetables and meats.
+ Ground mustard is a common ingredient in egg and cheese
  dishes, salad dressings and as a rub and seasoning for meat.

What is it?

Mustard seeds are cultivated from the mustard plant,
which is an annual vegetable related to broccoli, Brussels
sprouts and cabbage. Though there are about 40 known
varieties of mustard plants, the two principal types are
Brassica alba and Brassica juncea. Mustard plants grow
easily in temperate climates and are cultivated all over the
world. However, most of the mustard seed imported into
the U.S. is from Canada.

Try it this way:

+ Dredge chicken in prepared yellow or Dijon mustard, then
  sprinkle with mustard seed before baking.
+ Sprinkle mustard seed over prepared rice for a burst of flavor.
+ Stir a pinch of ground mustard into a cheese sauce; pour
  over asparagus spears, broccoli or pork chops.
+ Mix ground mustard into the filling for deviled eggs or into
  mayonnaise for a flavorful sandwich spread.

Nutmeg

What you'll find on the spice rack:

+ **Whole:** a glossy, brown seed with a piney, citrus-like aroma and sweet yet bitter taste, that grows inside an oval shell with wavy ridges, about the size of a peach pit
+ **Ground:** light brownish-red powder with a less potent spicy and sweet flavor than freshly grated whole nutmeg

Common uses:

+ Nutmeg is popular in the cuisines of Italy, the Caribbean, France, India, Germany, Scandinavia, Greece, Latin America, and the Middle East.
+ Nutmeg is often used in sweet foods and baked goods in conjunction with other spices, such as cinnamon, ginger and cloves.

What is it?

Nutmeg is the seed of a fruit from the tropical Myristica fragrans tree. It is perhaps nature's greatest packaging job. When ripe, the apricot-shaped fruit splits open to reveal the seed shell surrounded by a bright red lace covering that is scraped off to make the spice mace. The brittle shell opens up to expose the protected and flavorful nutmeg. It takes approximately 80 nutmegs to equal one pound.

Try it this way:

+ Sprinkle or grate a little nutmeg over egg nog, hot chocolate, cappuccino or pudding.
+ Include a dash of nutmeg to help season a bowl of tomato, split pea, chicken or black bean soup.

Onion

What you'll find on the spice rack:

+ *Flaked:* dehydrated onion bits dried in flake form until hard
+ *Ground:* off-white powder with an aromatic, spicy odor and mild onion flavor, also available in red and yellow onion powder

Common uses:

+ Dried onion flakes are used in many soup and dip recipes, as well as a substitute for fresh minced onion.
+ Onion powder is a popular seasoning for ground beef dishes, stews and chili.
+ A popular seasoning blend, onion salt, is a combination of two parts onion powder to one part salt.

What is it?

The onion family, Alliaceae, encompasses hundreds of varieties of onions. The majority of onion flakes and onion powder, however, is made from several varieties of pungent bulb onions, giving these seasonings a strong smell and flavoring.

Try it this way:

+ To impart an onion flavor when no fresh onions are available, substitute 1 tablespoon of dried onion flakes or 1 teaspoon of onion powder for every small onion in a recipe.
+ Stir a little onion powder or pinch of dried onion flakes into ground beef for taco filling, or into any gravy or savory sauce.
+ Whisk ½ teaspoon of onion powder with 2 tablespoons of olive oil and 2 teaspoons of vinegar for a quick salad dressing.

Oregano

What you'll find on the spice rack:

+ **Crushed:** green and bark-colored dried, crushed leaves with an earthy and pungent flavor and slight minty notes
+ **Ground:** greenish-brown powder that imparts a somewhat astringent mouth-feel

Common uses:

+ Oregano is often referred to as the pizza herb since it's a natural ingredient in any tomato-based sauce and makes a great addition to most Italian dishes.
+ Mexican or Cuban-style oregano is a popular ingredient in the spice blend chili powder.

What is it?

There are several types of oregano, each with their own flavor and strength. Hot and dry Mediterranean climates yield a robust, fully-flavored oregano with a slightly bitter, peppery taste. Cooler regions in Europe and North America yield a more delicate aroma and sweeter taste. The most popular subspecies, Origanum vulgare hirtum, is used in Greek and Italian-American cuisine, while L. graveolens, a less-minty and more hay-like subspecies, is used primarily in Mexican cuisine. At one time oregano and marjoram were thought to be the same plant.

Try it this way:

+ Add a pinch of crushed or ground oregano to hash browns or savory mashed potatoes, as well as omelets and quiches.
+ Sprinkle dried crushed oregano over a vegetable salad.
+ To make a quick homemade pizza sauce, stir together a 15-ounce can of tomato sauce, a 6-ounce can of tomato paste, 1 tablespoon of ground oregano and a pinch each of dried flaked garlic and paprika.

Paprika

What you'll find on the spice rack:

- *Ground:* bright reddish-orange powder with a sweet, rich taste or peppery bite, depending on the variety

Common uses:

- For a long time, paprika was merely considered a garnish for eggs, salads and hors d'oeuvres because of its often subdued flavor.
- Paprika is an essential ingredient for Paprikash and Goulash, popular Hungarian dishes.

What is it?

Paprika is made from the dried, ground pods of Capsicum annum, a sweet red pepper. Spanish paprika has a mildly sweet, rich taste, while the Hungarian varieties are more robust and peppery. Smoked paprika is made from three different peppers that are slowly smoked over oak and ground between stones resulting in a sweet, bittersweet and hot, vibrant red spice. Paprika is the only spice that is traded strictly as a ground product, but if the peppers are canned or bottled, they are known as pimento. Most paprika peppers are grown in South America, Hungary and Spain.

Try it this way:

- Rub a whole chicken inside and out with hot smoked paprika for a spicy roast chicken.
- Stir a little paprika into a prepared vinaigrette dressing; toss with salad or pasta.
- Sprinkle paprika over potatoes or homemade fries before baking.

Parsley

What you'll find on the spice rack:

+ *Flaked:* dark green dried, crushed leaves with a very mild aroma and flavor

Common uses:

+ Fresh parsley sprigs and even dried parsley flakes were once thought of as only a plate garnish to add color.
+ Parsley is often incorporated into egg dishes, soups and stocks to bring forth flavor.

What is it?

Parsley is the herb or spice from the bright green hardy biennial herb Petroselinum crispum, originating from Iran. It is now a popular ingredient in Middle Eastern, European and American cooking. While there are more than 40 varieties of parsley, only two are widely used in cooking: curled leaf, the usual garnish, and flat-leaf or Italian, used for a more intense, freshening flavor. It is believed the name parsley comes from the Greek word petros, meaning stone, because the plant was often found growing among rocks.

Try it this way:

+ Mix dried parsley flakes with olive oil and use as a mild marinade for seafood.
+ Mix dried parsley flakes into cream cheese, ricotta or cottage cheese before using in recipes or to make dips.
+ Stir dried parsley flakes into any pasta or potato salad.
+ Use dried parsley flakes to reduce the harshness of an over-garlicked dish without completely masking the flavor.

Pepper

What you'll find on the spice rack:

+ **Whole:** small dried round berries with a ridged, shriveled appearance and a sharp aroma and taste, known as peppercorns
+ **Ground:** peppercorns that have been ground into a coarse dust

Common uses:

+ Pepper is a universal table condiment and used to flavor all types of dishes in cuisines worldwide.
+ Pepper is often used in conjunction with eggs, vegetables, beef and chicken.
+ White pepper is often the preferable choice for flavoring lighter-colored dishes, such as cream sauces or mashed potatoes, where the use of black pepper would visibly stand out.

What is it?

Peppercorns are the dried berry fruit of the flowering vine called Piper nigrum in the Piperaceae family. The berries grow in clusters on vines that reach 30 feet tall or more. The same fruit produces black pepper, white pepper, green pepper, and red or pink pepper. The fruit is dark red when fully mature and contains a single seed.

Black pepper is produced from still-green unripe berries. The berries are cooked and dried to create black peppercorns. Green peppercorns are also plucked before ripening, then freeze-dried or soaked in a treatment with sulfur dioxide to preserve their green color. Pickled peppercorns are also green and preserved in brine or vinegar. White peppercorns are the seeds of the dried fruit. The fully-ripe berries are soaked in water until the fruit

(pepper continued...)

softens and decomposes, leaving behind the naked seeds. The rare pink or red peppercorns are made by preserving the ripe red berries in brine and vinegar. The pink peppercorns from the Piper nigrum vine are different from the more common dried pink berries from Peruvian pepper trees, Brazilian pepper trees or Baies rose plants.

It is arguable, but generally agreed, that black pepper has a more pungent flavor and sharp aroma, while white pepper is hotter, less subtle and mildly fermented. Mildest in flavor, it is often said that green pepper has a fresh taste while red pepper has a sweeter taste. Red peppercorns from plants other than the Piper nigrum have a slightly fruity flavor and are softer than true peppercorns. They should be crushed instead of ground through a pepper mill. Most of the world's pepper is grown in India, Indonesia, Malaysia and Brazil.

Try it this way:

+ For a stronger pepper taste, grind whole peppercorns over foods rather than using ground pepper.
+ Use pepper together with other ground spices as a dry rub for any meat.
+ Add a punch of spice to a bowl of soup or glass of tomato juice by stirring in a dash of pepper.

Poppy Seed

What you'll find on the spice rack:

+ **Whole:** seemingly round, tiny black seeds that are actually kidney shaped and slate-blue with a light nutty flavor

Common uses:

+ Poppy seeds are a popular addition to baked goods, such as poppy seed muffins, breads and bagels.
+ Poppy seeds are known to contain healthy oils and are used in many kinds of salads worldwide.

What is it?

The poppy seeds used for culinary purposes are harvested from ripened and dried seed pods from the Papaver somniferum plant, also known as the Oriental or opium poppy. This is the same decorative flower from which morphine, and ultimately, opium and heroin are created, though poppy seeds are harvested long after the capsule has lost its potential to produce a narcotic substance.

Try it this way:

+ To really bring forth a nutty flavor, toast or crush poppy seeds before using them in recipes. For example, toss some toasted poppy seeds with buttered noodles.
+ Sprinkle poppy seeds over a sweet fruit salad.
+ Stir a few poppy seeds into pancake or waffle batter.
+ Make a homemade exfoliating scrub by combining equal parts of olive oil and poppy seeds; stir in a few drops of orange essential oil. Massage the scrub into dry hands and feet; rinse with warm water.

Rosemary

What you'll find on the spice rack:

+ **Crushed:** needles removed from the branch and either crushed or dried whole, with a woodsy-pine aroma and fresh, bittersweet flavor

Common uses:

+ Rosemary is a popular ingredient in Italian and French cuisine, and often paired with lamb, pork, chicken and rabbit dishes.
+ Rosemary is often used in the seasoning blend herbes de Provence, as well as in a bouquet garni.

What is it?

Rosemary is a spiky evergreen bush that grows to an average height of 5 feet. Its needle-like pine boughs are harvested primarily in the former Yugoslavia region, France, Spain and Portugal. To use a fresh or dried whole sprig of rosemary, strip the needles from the branch by holding the tip and pulling down on the needle-like leaves in the opposite direction they are growing. Chop the leaves before stirring into a recipe. The name rosemary derives from the Latin name rosmarinus, which translates to *"dew of the sea"*.

Try it this way:

+ Mix dried rosemary with butter and fresh lemon juice; drizzle over baked fish or roasted red potatoes.
+ Steep a few whole dried rosemary leaves in a mug of hot water; let steep for a few minutes, strain and then drink as a calming tea.

Saffron

What you'll find on the spice rack:

+ **Whole:** deep reddish-orange delicate threads characterized by a bitter taste and hay-like fragrance, known to give food a rich golden-yellow hue

Common uses:

+ Saffron is common in rice and fish dishes around the world, and Spanish cooks consider it a must-have for making Paella and Arroz con Pollo.
+ Throughout history, saffron has been used in healing remedies, religious ceremonies and as a dye for fabrics.

What is it?

Saffron is the dried stigma of the perennial purple Saffron Crocus flower. It is the world's most expensive spice because the cultivation is very labor intensive. Each flower, which blooms for only two or three weeks in autumn, produces three reddish-orange stigmas. The flowers are picked by hand and the stigmas are plucked from each bloom, then cured over heat. It takes about 210,000 stigmas to make one pound of saffron, which can cost more than $800. Luckily, a little saffron goes a long way. Saffron flowers are native to Southwest Asia, however, Spain is now the world's largest grower and exporter of saffron.

Try it this way:

+ Soak a few saffron threads in water or milk before adding the spice and liquid to a recipe. This helps intensify the golden yellow color and brings out flavor.
+ Use saffron to season a potato or tomato-based casserole or soup.

Sage

What you'll find on the spice rack:

+ **Cut:** dried leaves that are cut down to a uniform size, described as a combination of rosemary, pine and mint with faint citrusy notes, more bitter than fresh sage or rubbed leaves
+ **Rubbed:** dried leaves that are delicately ground and rubbed, resulting in a unique, fluffy, almost cotton-like herb; the most popular form of sage

Common uses:

+ Sage is often used to season sausages, poultry and fish.
+ It is common to add sage to stuffing for poultry or pork. Recipes usually call for 1 or 2 teaspoons of minced sage per cup of stuffing.

What is it?

Sage is a shrub-like flowering plant from the mint family Lamiaceae. It is native to Mediterranean regions, but now cultivated in many parts of the world, including the Pacific coast of the U.S. More than 900 varieties of sage exist, but Dalmatian sage is believed to be the finest quality. Fresh or rubbed sage is far less bitter than dried sage, but a little goes a long way in any form. It is often added early in the cooking process so as not to overwhelm the dish and because it can withstand long cooking times. One variety, the hummingbird-attracting pineapple sage, is a lot sweeter and reflects a hint of pineapple in the aroma and taste.

Try it this way:

+ Sprinkle a little cut or rubbed sage over the cheese in a grilled cheese sandwich.
+ Stir a little cut or rubbed sage into batter or dough for corn bread, biscuits or scones.

Salt

What you'll find on the spice rack:

+ **Unrefined:** natural sea salts, each with different mineralities, resulting in unique flavors from region to region

+ **Refined:** salt that has been refined to purify it and improve its storage and handling characteristics, such as the addition of anti-caking agents, and from which most minerals have been removed. Only 17.5% of refined salt production is used for food and culinary purposes

+ **Iodized:** salt (often table salt) to which a small amount of potassium iodide has been added as an important dietary supplement to reduce iodine deficiency in humans, a common cause of thyroid gland problems

Common uses:

+ Salt has more than 14,000 known uses, with only a small percentage of those uses involved with food.

+ The greatest single use for salt is in the production of chemicals, such as chlorine and hydrochloric acid.

+ For thousands of years, salt has been used to aid the preservation of food.

+ Humans and animals require sodium and chloride, both which are nutrients found in salt, in order to live and stay healthy.

(salt continued...)

What is it?

Salt is neither an herb nor a spice; it's a mineral that is essential to the functioning of the human body. Salt is either obtained by evaporating sea water, resulting in sea salt, or it is mined, diluted, filtered and evaporated by steam or direct heat. Next, the many types of salts harvested are made available in different grades. The most common form, table salt, is considered regular grade, but it is also available in fine grade, rock form and coarse Kosher. Salt is often mixed with other spices and herbs to create seasoning blends, the most popular of which are celery salt, onion salt and garlic salt. These are just a few of the popular salts used for culinary purposes:

+ *Sea salt* is a broad term that refers to any unrefined salt derived directly from the ocean or sea. Proponents of sea salt swear by its pure, bright, clean flavor, as well as the subtle flavors incorporated by trace minerals it contains.

+ *Fleur de Sel,* literally "flower of the sea", is a premier condiment and finishing sea salt. It is ideal for sprinkling over salads, cooked fresh vegetables and grilled meats.

+ *Hawaiian sea salt,* also called Alaea or Alae, comprises volcanic baked red clay added to sea salt to enrich it with iron oxide. It is perfect for seasoning prime rib and pork loin.

+ *Coarse salt* is a broad term that refers to larger-grained salt crystals. It is preferred by many professional chefs because it resists caking and is easy to measure with their fingers. It is used for rubs on meat or fish, as well as flavoring soups and pasta.

Savory

What you'll find on the spice rack:

+ *Crushed:* brownish-green dried leaves, similar to thyme, with slightly sharp, minty, green and medicinal notes
+ *Ground:* very light tannish-green powder with a somewhat peppery flavor and minty thyme background

Common uses:

+ In France, it is common to marinate goat cheese rounds in olive oil and savory.
+ Savory is a common ingredient in stuffings, soup mixes and condiments.

What is it?

The two varieties of savory, summer and winter, are from very different plants. Summer savory is an annual herb with slender branches and a more delicate flavor. Winter savory is a shrubby perennial with wood branches. Summer savory is far more popular for cooking or using fresh and, unless grown at home, it can be assumed that nearly all commercial forms of savory are dried and made from the summer variety. Bees are very attracted to the flowers of the savory plants, and at one time, crushed savory leaves were a common reliever for bee stings.

Try it this way:

+ Tomatoes pair exceptionally well with savory. Try using savory in place of or in addition to the basil in a tomato dish or sauce.
+ Stir a little savory into a dish of baked or refried beans, or use it to season a bean soup.

Sesame Seed

What you'll find on the spice rack:

+ **Whole:** small tear-drop shaped seeds that come in a variety of colors, from cream-white to charcoal-black, with a nutty, oily, sometimes bitter flavor

Common uses:

+ A popular complement to many grains, sesame seeds are often baked into crackers or found on top of bagels and hamburger buns.
+ In Japan, sesame seeds are a common ingredient in salads, baked snacks and sushi-style foods.
+ Tahini, an essential ingredient for Middle Eastern dishes such as hummus and baba ghanoush, is made from sesame seeds.

What is it?

Sesame seeds are gathered from the annual flowering plant Sesamum indicum, which grows 2 to 3 feet tall with delicate tubular white to purple flowers. The seeds are available either hulled (the milky white versions that are more valued in the West and Middle East) or unhulled (the brown, black or even red versions that are prized in the Far East). Of the approximate four billion pounds of sesame seeds produced each year, most of them are pressed into sesame oil. To intensify the nutty flavor, toast sesame seeds before using them in a recipe (see page 4).

Try it this way:

+ Combine toasted sesame seeds with rice vinegar, soy sauce and crushed garlic; use as a dressing for salads or noodles.
+ Sprinkle toasted sesame seeds over steamed vegetables or a crumb-topped casserole.

Star Anise

What you'll find on the spice rack:

+ **Whole:** rust-colored, hard, dried flower with six to twelve (typically eight) boat-shaped pods, each of which contains a hard seed, with a strong licorice-like aroma and taste, very similar to, but more powerful than, aniseed or fennel

+ **Ground:** reddish-brown powder made from grinding whole star anise

Common uses:

+ Star anise is very popular in Chinese and Indian cuisine, where it is a major component of the spice blends Chinese five spice powder and garam masala.

+ Historically, star anise has been used to freshen breath or for the treatment of colic and nausea.

What is it?

Star anise is the beautiful fruit of the Illicium verum, a small native evergreen tree of southwest China. The star-shaped fruits are harvested before ripening and then dried. Star anise contains anethole, the same ingredient which gives the unrelated aniseed its flavor. Because of their similar flavors, the cheaper star anise can often be substituted for aniseed. One crushed star anise equals about ½ teaspoon of crushed aniseed. India and Syria are the largest producers of star anise.

Try it this way:

+ Add a whole star anise to a roast or other meat dish that is slow-simmered for several hours.

+ Drop a whole star anise into a brew of boiled or sun-steeped tea; sweeten the tea and remove the star anise before serving over ice.

Tamarind

What you'll find on the spice rack:

+ **Block:** dark brown, soft, compressed and dried bricks of tamarind pulp, mostly which have the seeds and strings removed; the consistency of moist modeling clay, needs to be reconstituted in water to make tamarind juice, a thick fruit nectar

+ **Concentrate:** tangy, prune-like, ready-to-use pulp that is the consistency of jam, also called tamarind paste

Common uses:

+ Throughout history, the medicinal uses of tamarind include helping to relieve sore throats or digestive problems, reducing malaria fever, alleviating sunstroke and alcoholic intoxication, and warding off night demons.

+ Tamarind is a popular ingredient in curries, chutneys, sauces, soups, sorbets and drinks.

What is it?

Tamarind is made from the pulp of large fruit pods that hang from the Tamarindus indica, a tropical tree native to Africa. Each reddish-brown, curved pod contains several large seeds encased by moist, sticky, dark brown flesh that ranges from being very sweet to very sour. The hard green pulp harvested from young fruit is very tart and acidic. It is most often used as a component of savory dishes. The ripened fruit is sweeter, yet still distinctively sour, and can be used in sweetened drinks and desserts. Tamarind trees are now found in all tropical and near-tropical areas, including South Florida, where it is grown in parks and along roadsides.

Try it this way:

+ Stir reconstituted tamarind water or tamarind paste into a peppery, savory sauce; serve with seafood.

Tarragon

What you'll find on the spice rack:

+ **Crushed:** khaki-colored dried leaves with a licorice-like, minty, earthy flavor and aroma

Common uses:

+ Very popular in French cuisine, tarragon is an essential ingredient in Béarnaise sauce, tarragon vinegar and Dijon mustard.
+ Tarragon is widely used in perfumes, soaps, cosmetics, condiments and liqueurs.

What is it?

Tarragon is a perennial herb popularized by French cuisine and introduced in the U.S. in the early 19th century. It is from the Asteraceae family and related to wormwood. When wormwood was given the nickname "The Old Woman", tarragon followed suit with its own common name: "The Old Man". Tarragon, with an intense licorice, slightly minty flavor, is noted as one of the most dominating herbs. Therefore, it is often used sparingly or simply as a garnish, or added in small doses at the end of cooking to make the best use of its flavor.

Try it this way:

+ Add dried tarragon to an omelet along with parsley flakes and dried basil or thyme.
+ Stir ¼ teaspoon of dried tarragon into ¼ cup of mayonnaise, ¼ cup of butter, ¼ cup of sour cream or ¼ cup of yogurt; spread over sandwiches or use in place of these regular ingredients in recipes.

Thyme

What you'll find on the spice rack:

+ **Dried:** grayish-green tiny needle-like leaves characterized by a minty-green, hay-like flavor and aroma with musty notes

Common uses:

+ The phrase "when in doubt, use thyme" has caused this popular ingredient to be paired successfully with everything from stuffing and meat to stews and vegetables.
+ Thyme is a popular ingredient in many spice blends, including a bouquet garni and herbes de Provence, as well as the Middle Eastern blend, zahtar.

What is it?

Thyme is an aromatic perennial herb from the Lamiaceae family, and native to Europe, North Africa and Asia. It is one of the most popular herbs in many cultures, including American, French, Greek, Italian, Lebanese, Spanish, Turkish and Persian. Thyme retains its flavor after drying better than many other herbs. Therefore, use only half or one-third of the required amount of fresh thyme when substituting with dried. Most thyme is imported from Spain, but it is a fairly hardy plant and easy to grow at home.

Try it this way:

+ Add a sprinkling of dried thyme to a slow-cooked meat dish.
+ Sprinkle dried thyme over any dish that includes potatoes, eggs, tomatoes, beans or beef.
+ Use dried thyme as a pizza seasoning or in savory, meaty stir-fry recipes.

Turmeric

What you'll find on the spice rack:

+ **Ground:** bright orangey-yellow powder made from the dried roots of the plant; described as a combination of ginger and pepper flavors with an earthy, mustard-like scent

Common uses:

+ Ground turmeric is a common ingredient in curry blends and used to add color and flavor to mustard condiments.
+ The pumpkin-orange tubular roots of turmeric are often used as a coloring agent for baked products, beverages, cheeses, margarine, ice cream, yogurt, orange juice, biscuits, popcorn flavoring, cereals, sauces and gelatins.

What is it?

Turmeric is an herbaceous perennial plant from the ginger family, Zingiberaceae. Its stem and roots (or rhizomes) are harvested, boiled, dried and ground to make turmeric powder, a popular seasoning in South Asian cuisine. More than 90% of the world's supply of turmeric comes from India.

Try it this way:

+ Turmeric is known for masking a fishy smell. Use it to season fresh fish before cooking or in sauces served with seafood.
+ Add some ground turmeric to homemade pasta dough for added color and flavor.
+ A sprinkling of turmeric will add good flavor and color to any dish containing chicken, beef, cauliflower, squash or lentils.
+ A spoonful of turmeric added to a water-cooled radiator will plug a leak almost magically.

Vanilla Bean

What you'll find on the spice rack:

+ **Whole:** dark brown, dried fruit pods that contain a thick pulp with a prune-like, floral, rum-like, rich flavor and highly aromatic, exceptionally sweet fragrance

Common uses:

+ Vanilla is an essential flavor added to many baked goods, desserts and perfumes.
+ The scent and flavor of vanilla was considered an aphrodisiac in many cultures.

What is it?

Vanilla beans are the fruit of climbing perennial orchids, mainly the Vanilla planifolia, and native to Central America. Today, vanilla beans are cultivated in Mexico, Madagascar, Tahiti and Indonesia. Amazingly, the fruit pods have no flavor or aroma when harvested. It is not until after the drying and sweating process that the pods ferment and release their familiar scent and taste. Vanilla plants and beans are also used to produce the most popular extract flavor and a very desirable essential oil. To scrape the seeds from a vanilla bean, lay the bean flat over a piece of parchment paper. Use a paring knife to split the bean lengthwise; scrape the seeds from both sides of the pod.

Try it this way:

+ Make your own vanilla sugar: add a few whole beans to a sugar bowl and allow it to sit for a few weeks. The sugar will absorb the rich flavor and take on a wonderful scent. Use it in coffee, tea, cocoa, baking or sprinkled over toast.
+ Add the pulp from a vanilla bean to a dessert sauce, custard, syrup, fruit salad or batch of homemade ice cream.

Cajun Seasoning

What you'll find on the spice rack:

+ **Ground:** brownish-red spicy powder blend, similar in consistency to seasoning salt

Common uses:

+ Cajun seasoning is essential to the popular blackening method of cooking chicken, catfish, shrimp and vegetables.
+ Cajun seasoning is known for bringing out true Cajun or Louisiana flavor in poultry, seafood, meat, corn bread, beans and other vegetables.

What is it?

Cajun seasoning is a spice blend made by combining salt, pepper, garlic powder, onion powder, chili powder and/or cayenne pepper. Sometimes paprika, marjoram, fennel seed, dried oregano, dried parsley and dried thyme are added to the mix. Also called Creole Seasoning or Cajun Blackening Powder, this spice blend is used to add heat and spiciness to a recipe.

Try it this way:

+ Try sprinkling a little Cajun seasoning over popcorn, rice or on toasted nuts for a unique kick.
+ Stir some Cajun seasoning into ground beef to make burgers or grilled chicken for sandwiches.

Chili Powder

What you'll find on the spice rack:

+ **Ground:** very spicy, fine powder blend ranging in color from orangey-yellow to deep, dark red

Common uses:

+ Chili powder is an essential ingredient in almost every version of chili con carne, the stew-like dish referred to in America simply as chili.
+ Chili powder is often used in India for the preparation of curry dishes, as well as being a favorite in Mexican and South American cuisine.

What is it?

Chili powder is a spice blend made by combining dried chili peppers, cumin, oregano, garlic powder and salt. Sometimes black pepper, cinnamon, cloves, coriander, mace, nutmeg or turmeric are added to the mix. Chile pepper or powder with an "e" refers to a spice made simply by grinding dried chili peppers. The most common peppers used to make chili powder are red peppers or cayenne peppers, however, almost any hot pepper can be used, including ancho, Chipotle, New Mexico and pasilla chili peppers.

Try it this way:

+ Use chili powder as a rub for steak, fish and chicken before broiling, baking or grilling.
+ Make a spicy hamburger by mixing chili powder by hand into any ground meat.

SPICE BLEND

Chinese Five Spice

What you'll find on the spice rack:

+ **Ground:** reddish-brown to deep brown powder blend, with the dominant flavor and aroma coming from the star anise

Common uses:

+ A popular flavoring for lamb, pork, beef and tofu dishes, Chinese five spice powder is generally considered too overpowering for most vegetable dishes.
+ Chinese five spice powder is used in most recipes for beef stew and Cantonese roast duck.

What is it?

Chinese five spice powder is a spice blend made by combining star anise, clove, fennel, cinnamon and Szechuan peppercorns. Sometimes it is seven spice powder, when cardamom, dried ginger or licorice root are added to the mix. This mix is the only common spice blend in Chinese cuisine, and the formula is based on the Chinese philosophy of achieving a yin and yang balance by including the five basic flavors: sweet, sour, bitter, pungent and salty.

Try it this way:

+ Include Chinese five spice powder in a dry rub or simmering liquid for any kind of ribs.
+ Add a pinch of Chinese five spice powder to lend flavor to a soup or stir-fry.

Curry Powder

What you'll find on the spice rack:

* **_Ground:_** a complex pulverized blend of up to 20 spices, herbs and seeds, typically deep golden yellow in color, usually a hot spicy flavor that can be musky, earthy, or even sweet

Common uses:

* Curry blends are used in Indian cooking in the same way salt and pepper are used in American cuisine.
* It is believed by many that curry blends help stimulate organs, improve eyesight and clear up the skin.

What is it?

The Southern Indian word "khari", from which "curry" is derived, refers to a sauce of any kind. There are millions of curry flavors in India, and most Indian cooks have their own mixtures for different recipes. Despite this, curry powder, as it is known in the Western world, has a pretty standardized taste. It was developed by the British, who wished to take the taste of Indian food home after their colonial rule of India ended. Most curry powders include coriander, turmeric, cumin and fenugreek. Sometimes additional spices, such as allspice, cardamom, celery seed, cinnamon, cloves, coriander, cumin, fennel seed, ginger, garlic, mace, mustard seed, nutmeg and pepper are added to the mix.

Try it this way:

* Stir a pinch of curry powder into a cold chicken or pasta salad; mix well.
* Use curry powder to season rice, couscous, seafood and stir-fry.

GARAM MASALA

Garam Masala

What you'll find on the spice rack:

+ **Ground:** an intricate crushed blend of up to 12 spices, herbs and seeds, typically light to golden brown in color, usually a hot spicy flavor though less intense than most other curry powders

Common uses:

+ Garam masala is mostly used to enhance the flavor of meat and savory dishes.
+ Many cooks will sprinkle a pinch of garam masala over soup, stew or a vegetable dish just before serving.

What is it?

Garam masala is a specific curry blend popular in Indian, Bangladeshi and Pakistani cuisine. Its literal translation means "hot spice", although garam refers to hot in terms of temperature, not spice. Typically, garam masala is a spice blend made by combining caraway, cardamom, cinnamon, cloves, roasted cumin, and nutmeg or mace. Sometimes chili pepper, garlic, ginger, sesame seeds, mustard seeds, turmeric, coriander, star anise and fennel are added to the mix. Garam masala is usually added at the end of cooking to retain most of its flavor.

Try it this way:

+ Brush ears of grilled corn with butter, then sprinkle with a little garam masala.
+ Sprinkle garam masala over a squash before roasting, or into a bowl of pumpkin soup just before serving.

Herbes de Provence

What you'll find on the spice rack:

+ *Crushed:* green, tan, sometimes purple, aromatic blend of crushed leaves and flowers

Common uses:

+ Herbes de Provence is popular for flavoring grilled meats and seafood.
+ Typically, herbes de Provence are mixed into oil early in the cooking process in order to infuse the most flavor into the foods.

What is it?

Herbes de Provence, also called Provençal herbs, is a spice blend developed in the 1970s in the Provence region of southeastern France. Most blends contain basil, bay leaf, marjoram, rosemary, savory and thyme, though the proportions vary by manufacturer. Some blends also include orange zest and/or lavender flowers. Traditionally, herbes de Provence is sold in terra cotta jars or small crocks.

Try it this way:

+ Mix herbes de Provence with olive oil; brush over chicken, turkey, fish or potatoes before grilling or roasting.
+ When grilling, add a couple pinches of herbes de Provence to hot coals for a nice flavor and aroma.
+ Stir herbes de Provence into a pasta or pizza sauce.
+ Combine two parts mayonnaise, one part Dijon mustard, a little champagne vinegar and a spinkling of herbes de Provence; use to season a potato salad.

Italian Seasoning

What you'll find on the spice rack:

+ **Crushed:** light green and brown blend of dried, crushed leaves with a savory aroma and taste
+ **Ground:** grayish-green powder made by pulverizing the crushed form of Italian seasoning

Common uses:

+ Italian seasoning is a popular addition to many Italian dishes, include sauces, pizzas, meatballs, lasagna and spaghetti.

What is it?

Italian seasoning is a spice blend made by combining basil, marjoram, oregano, rosemary, sage, savory and thyme. Sometimes red pepper flakes and onion powder are added to the mix. Italian seasoning represents many of the traditional spices used in Italian cuisine.

Try it this way:

+ Drizzle sliced fresh tomatoes with olive oil and a sprinkling of crushed Italian seasoning.
+ Mix 1½ teaspoons crushed Italian seasoning with ½ cup softened butter and ¼ cup grated Parmesan cheese; spread over toasted French bread or baked potatoes.
+ Sprinkle ground Italian seasoning over salads, sub sandwiches, steamed vegetables or cooked pasta.
+ Add a pinch of Italian seasoning to a cheesy egg dish, such as an omelet, egg bake or quiche.
+ Season a basic oil-and-vinegar dressing with Italian seasoning. Add 1 teaspoon per every 1 cup of dressing.

Jerk Seasoning

What you'll find on the spice rack:

+ **Ground:** hot and spicy, thick seasoning blend that is typically deep, dark red in color

Common uses:

+ Jerk seasoning is essential for achieving the jerk style of cooking that is native to Jamaica.
+ Chicken and pork are two of the most common meats seasoned with jerk seasoning.

What is it?

Jerk seasoning, also called Jamaican jerk spice, is a spice blend made by combining allspice and the dried ground form of spicy Scotch bonnet peppers, some of the hottest chile peppers available. Sometimes cloves, cinnamon, scallions, nutmeg, thyme and/or garlic are added to the mix. Typically, jerk seasoning is dry-rubbed directly onto meat or blended with a liquid to create a marinade.

Try it this way:

+ Season a pork rump roast or whole chicken with jerk seasoning. Wearing plastic gloves, cut shallow scores in the surface of the pork and rub all over with jerk seasoning, or rub the seasoning under the skin of a whole chicken. Wrap the meat tightly in plastic wrap and refrigerate overnight. When ready to prepare, slow-roast the meat for several hours over low heat.
+ To make a jerk marinade for meat or seafood, mix jerk seasoning with soy sauce, lime juice, orange juice, oil, rum or water.

Lemon Pepper Seasoning

What you'll find on the spice rack:

+ **Ground:** coarse, zesty seasoning blend characterized by the flavors of lemon zest and black peppercorns

Common uses:

+ Originally, lemon pepper was used exclusively as a seasoning for baked, broiled, grilled or fried seafood.
+ More recently, recipes for poultry, pork and veal have included lemon pepper.

What is it?

Lemon pepper seasoning is a spice blend made by combining dried ground lemon zest and ground black peppercorns. Sometimes salt, garlic, onion and/or celery seed are added to the mix. Though its origins are unknown, lemon pepper seasoning was probably created as a quick-fix seasoning blend that combines flavors that traditionally pair well with and bring forth new flavor in fish and other seafood.

Try it this way:

+ Stir a pinch of lemon pepper seasoning into canned chunk tuna.
+ Mix some lemon pepper seasoning into plain hummus or other bean dips.
+ Sprinkle lemon pepper seasoning over pork chops and press into the meat with a fork; sauté, grill, fry or bake.
+ Add a pinch of lemon pepper seasoning to an egg dish, such as an omelet, egg bake, quiche or scrambled eggs.

Pickling Spice

What you'll find on the spice rack:

- **Whole:** whole or coarsely chopped mixture of various spices, herbs and seeds that are both sweet and tangy, used to give pickles their characteristic flavor

Common uses:

- The primary use for pickling spice is to add flavor to various foods, primarily pickles, during the pickling process.
- Pickling spice has been used to add complex flavor to braised meats, stews, beans and rice dishes.

What is it?

Pickling spice is a blend of almost any number and kind of spice available. Most commercial blends of pickling spice include allspice, bay leaves, cardamom, cinnamon, cloves, coriander, ginger, mustard seed and peppercorns, though almost any kind of spice could be used.

Try it this way:

- To make a pickling sachet at home, place 1 or 2 tablespoons of pickling spice in the center of a coffee filter or piece of cheesecloth; close with kitchen twine. Add the sachet to slow-simmering or slow cooker soups, sauces and meat dishes; remove before serving.
- Add 3 tablespoons of pickling spice to each quart of water used when steaming 1 to 2 pounds of shrimp.

Spice Blend

When it comes to seasoning your food, you have hundreds upon thousands of possibilities. This book has provided an overview and suggestions for using the most popular spices, dried herbs and spice blends that are widely available. But you don't have to stop there...

You can create many more spicing options by making your *own* blends. This will allow you to tailor your seasonings exactly to your liking, and it will give your food a distinction that is all your own!

Start by mixing small amounts of various spices and dried herbs in a bowl. (If you prefer a powdered blend, you might want to invest in a spice grinder, which is a lot like a coffee grinder, only smaller.) Taste and smell your blend. Don't forget you can always stir in a little salt, pepper or sugar. To give a good indication of what your blend will taste like when cooked with food, heat a little oil or butter in a sauté pan over medium-low heat; stir in one or two pinches of your blend. Cook and stir the mixture to open up the flavor and aroma of the spices. Spread some of the warmed blend on a cracker or piece of bread. Continue to adjust your blend until you are satisfied with your masterpiece! Store the dry mixture in an airtight container with a tight-fitting lid.

Gift 'em

Spice up the lives of your family and friends by giving them a small jar or container of your homemade spice blend. Attach a printed card that provides suggestions for how to use your custom blend.

Most of all, have fun exploring all the possibilities that are right there in your spice rack. Remember, variety is the spice of life — so give yours lots of flavor!